My Baptismal Covenants

(Renewed Each Time I Partake of the Sacrament)

At Baptism I Covenant with the Lord to:

1. Come into the fold of God (become a member of the Church of Jesus Christ).

2. Be called his son or daughter (take upon me the name of Christ).

3. Bear others' burdens, that they may be light; mourn with those that mourn; and comfort those in need of comfort (help others).

4. Stand as a witness of God at all times and in all things and in all places (testify of Christ and set a good example at all times).

5. Serve God and keep his commandments.

When I Keep My Baptismal Covenants the Lord Covenants to:

1. Forgive my sins.

2. Pour his Spirit more abundantly upon me (give me the companionship of the Holy Ghost).

3. Redeem me that I might be numbered with those of the first resurrection and have eternal life (permit me to enter the celestial kingdom to live with Heavenly Father and Jesus Christ).

Baptism

WRITTEN by Karen Dixon Merrell

ARTWORK by Gary Kapp

ISBN 0-87747-559-8

Our Heavenly Father loves us and gives us commandments so that we can be happy.

One of Heavenly Father's commandments is that we should be baptized.

Baptism opens the door so that we can someday live with Heavenly Father again.

Children should be baptized when they are eight years old.

When children are eight they become accountable. This means they should know how to choose right from wrong, and they are responsible for their choices.

Older people who didn't know about Heavenly Father's commandments are taught by the missionaries and are also baptized.

Many people died before hearing about
Heavenly Father's Church and were
not baptized. We are baptized for these
people in the temples.

When we are baptized we promise to keep all of Heavenly Father's commandments.

If we break our promise we should be sorry, and we should not do it again. We should also ask our Father in heaven to forgive us.

In the Bible we read that Jesus was baptized by John the Baptist in the River Jordan.

John the Baptist had the priesthood, which is the authority to do special things for our Father in heaven.

Many years later this same John gave the priesthood to Joseph Smith so that he could baptize too.

The man who baptizes you must have this same priesthood.

When you are baptized you wear white clothes.

You might be baptized in a church building, at a place called a font.

Or you can be baptized in a river or a lake or some other nice place where there is enough water.

The man who baptizes you says a special prayer.

Then he puts you under the water and lifts you up again.

Then you are confirmed a member of Heavenly Father's Church by men who also have the priesthood.

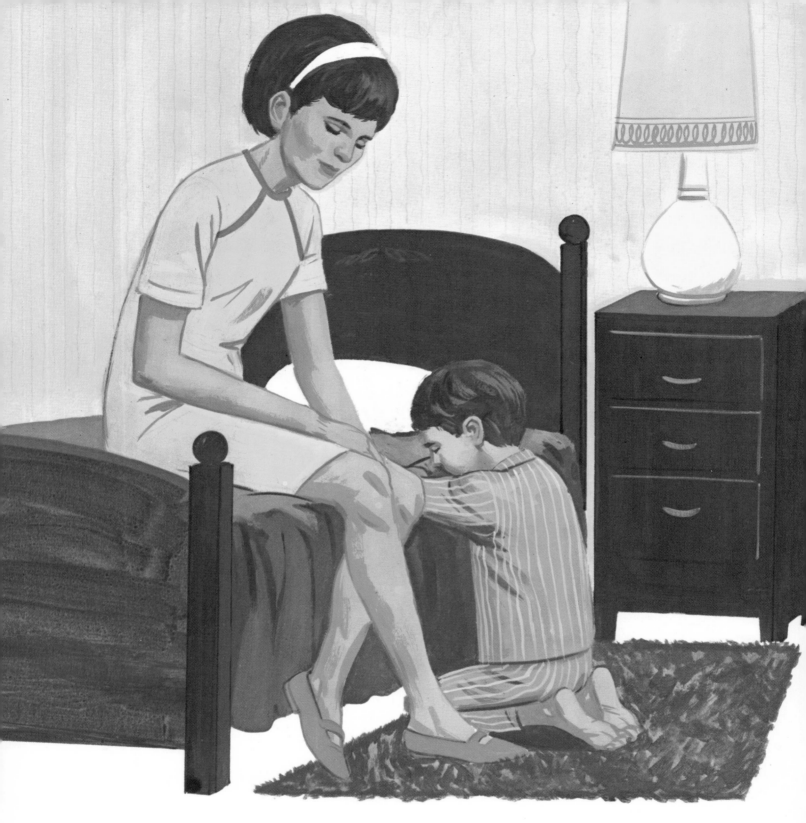

When you are confirmed you are given the gift of the Holy Ghost. You can then receive special blessings from your Heavenly Father.

The day when you are baptized will be one of the most important days of your life.

Ask your father and mother to teach you
what you should know so that you will
be ready for your baptism day.